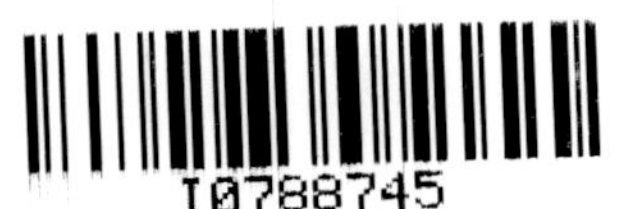

Coloring book for adults and kids amazing sheep design

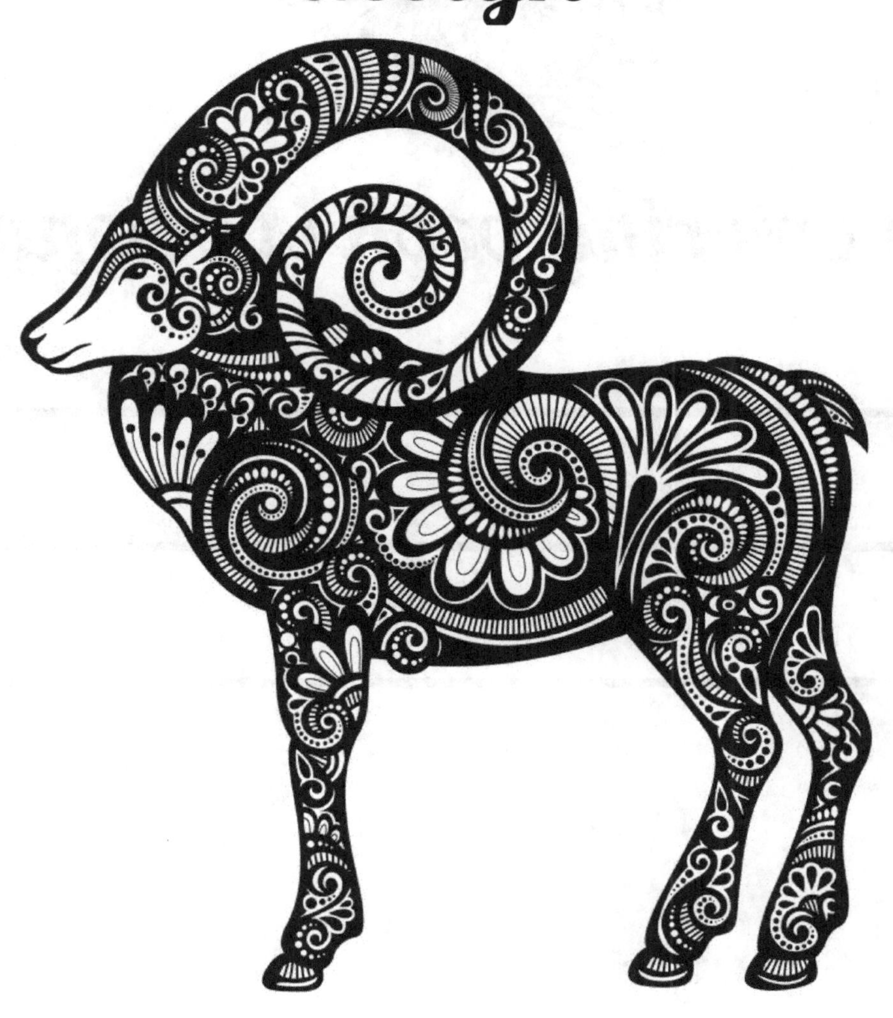

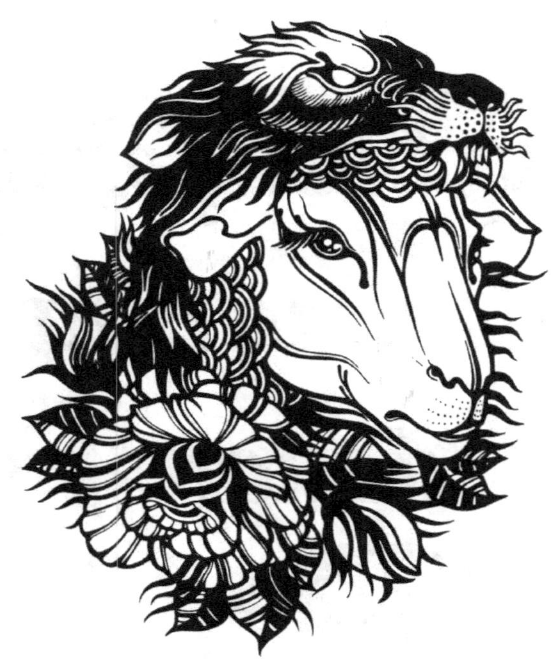

This coloring book is belongs to

____

____

____

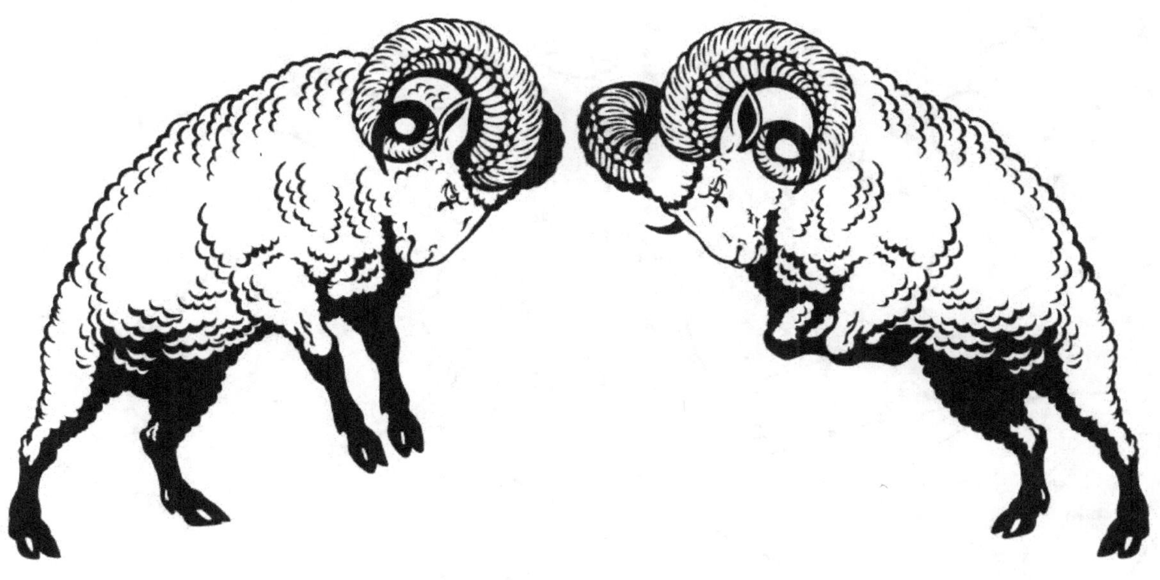

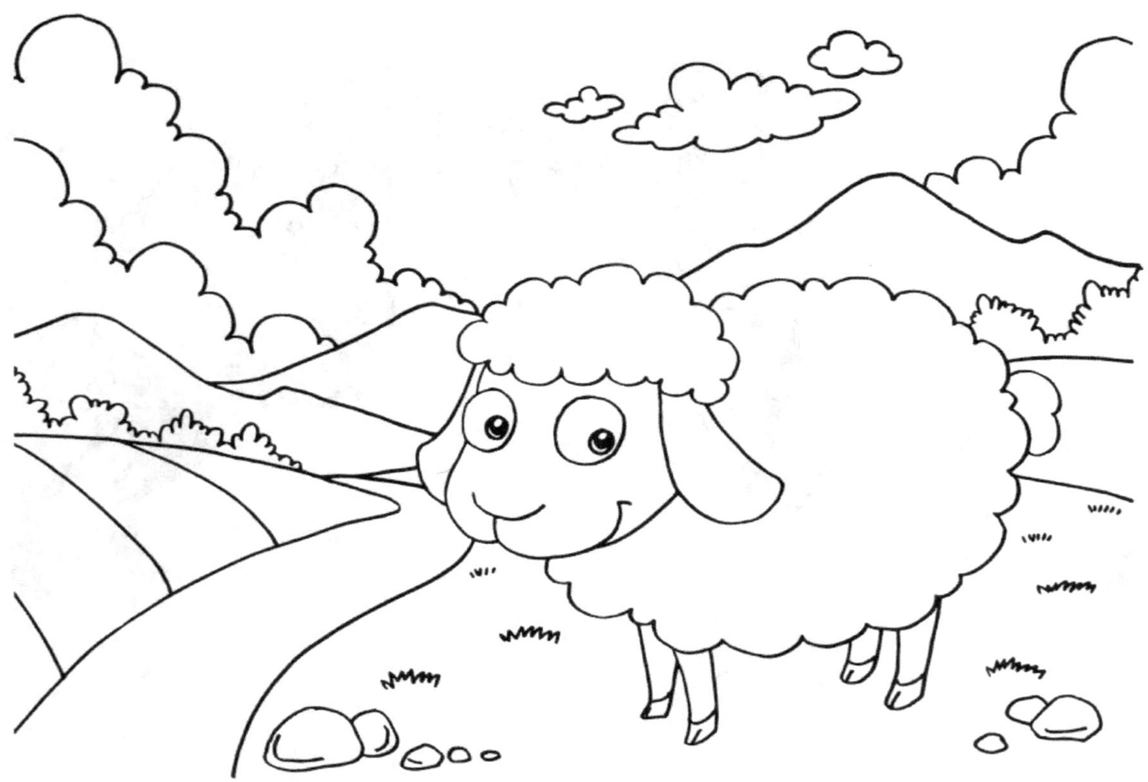

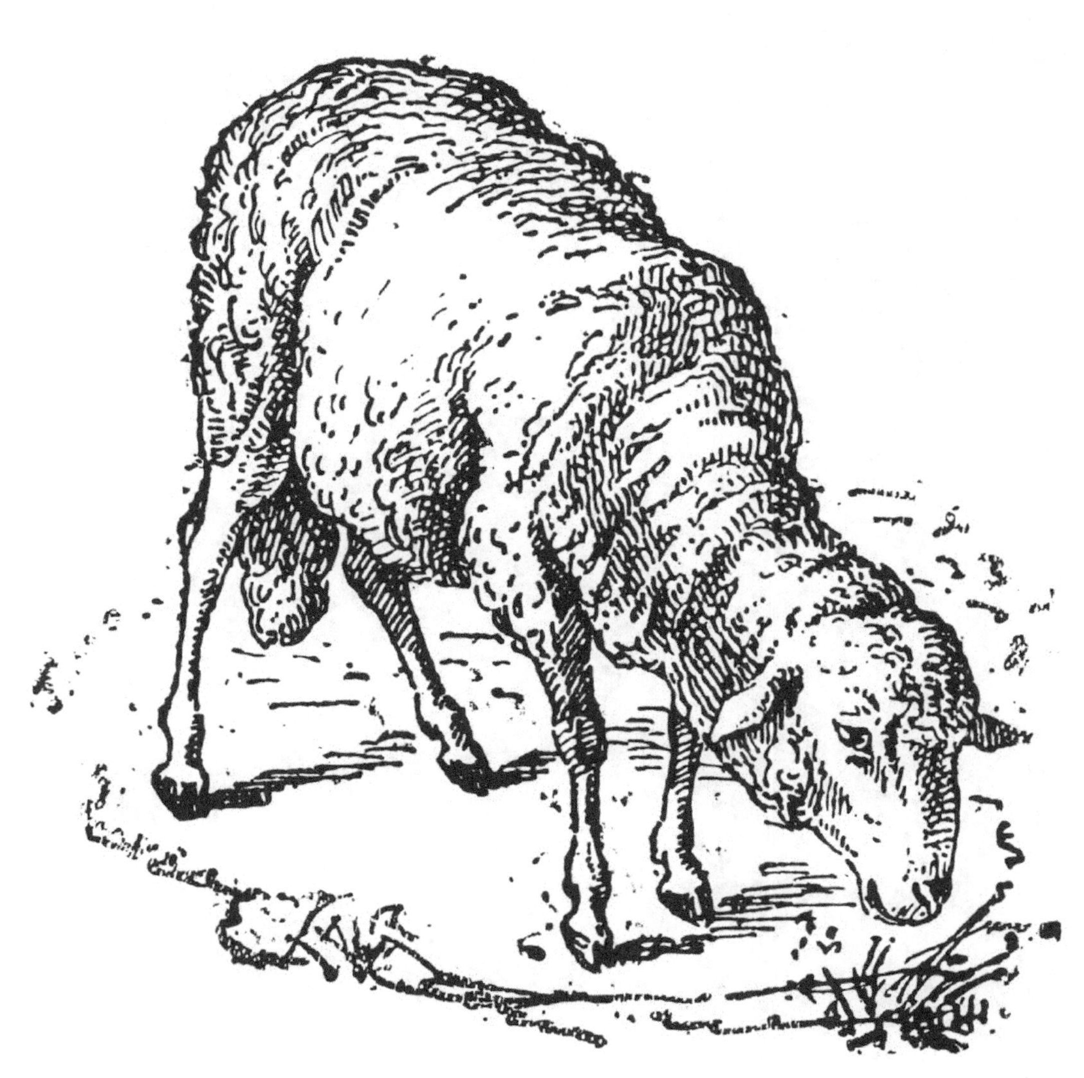

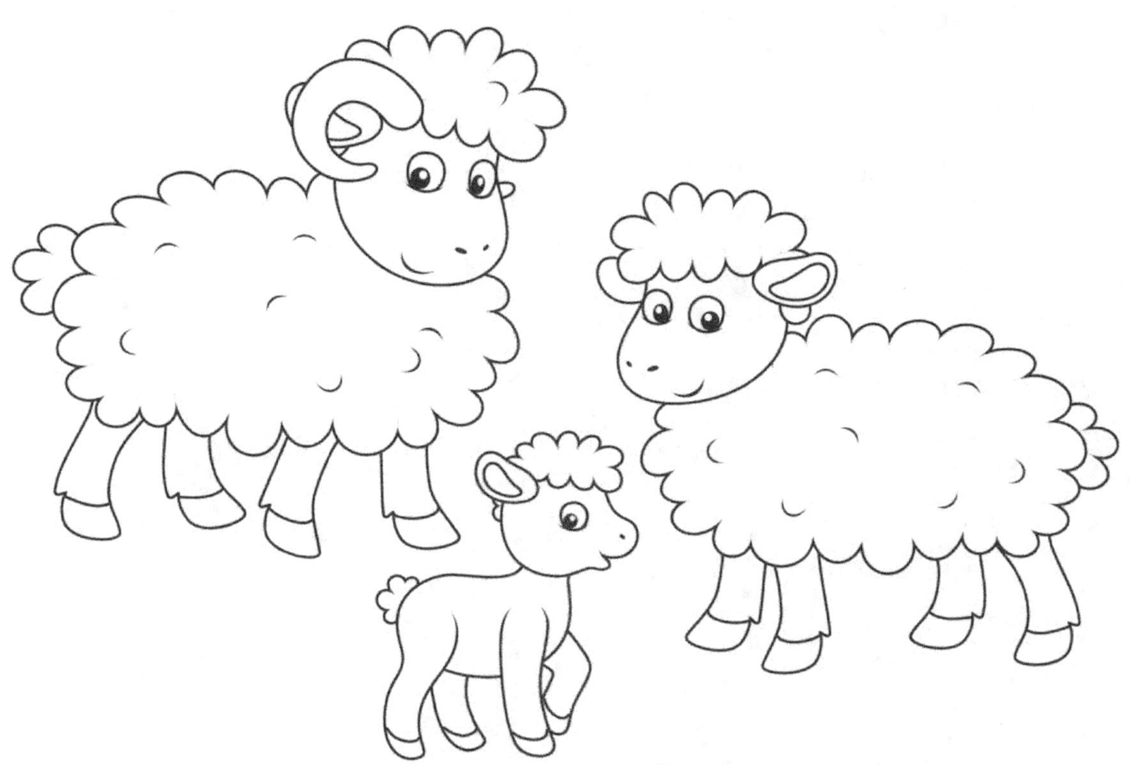

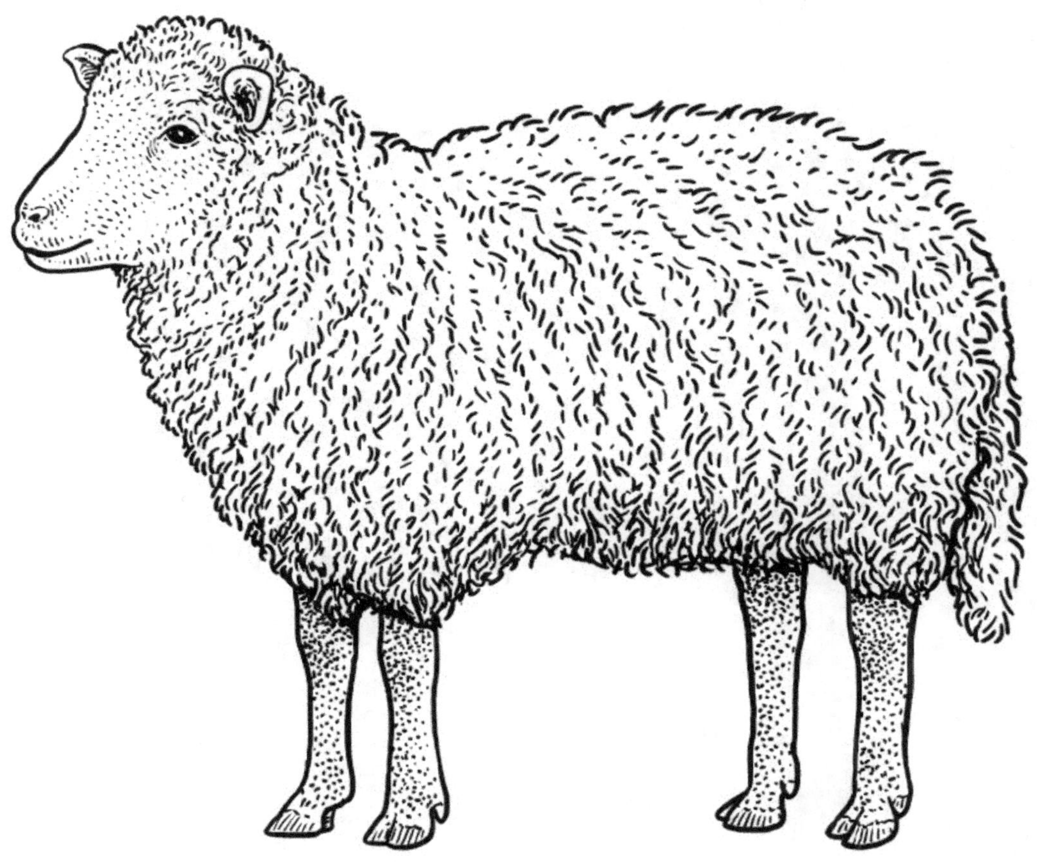

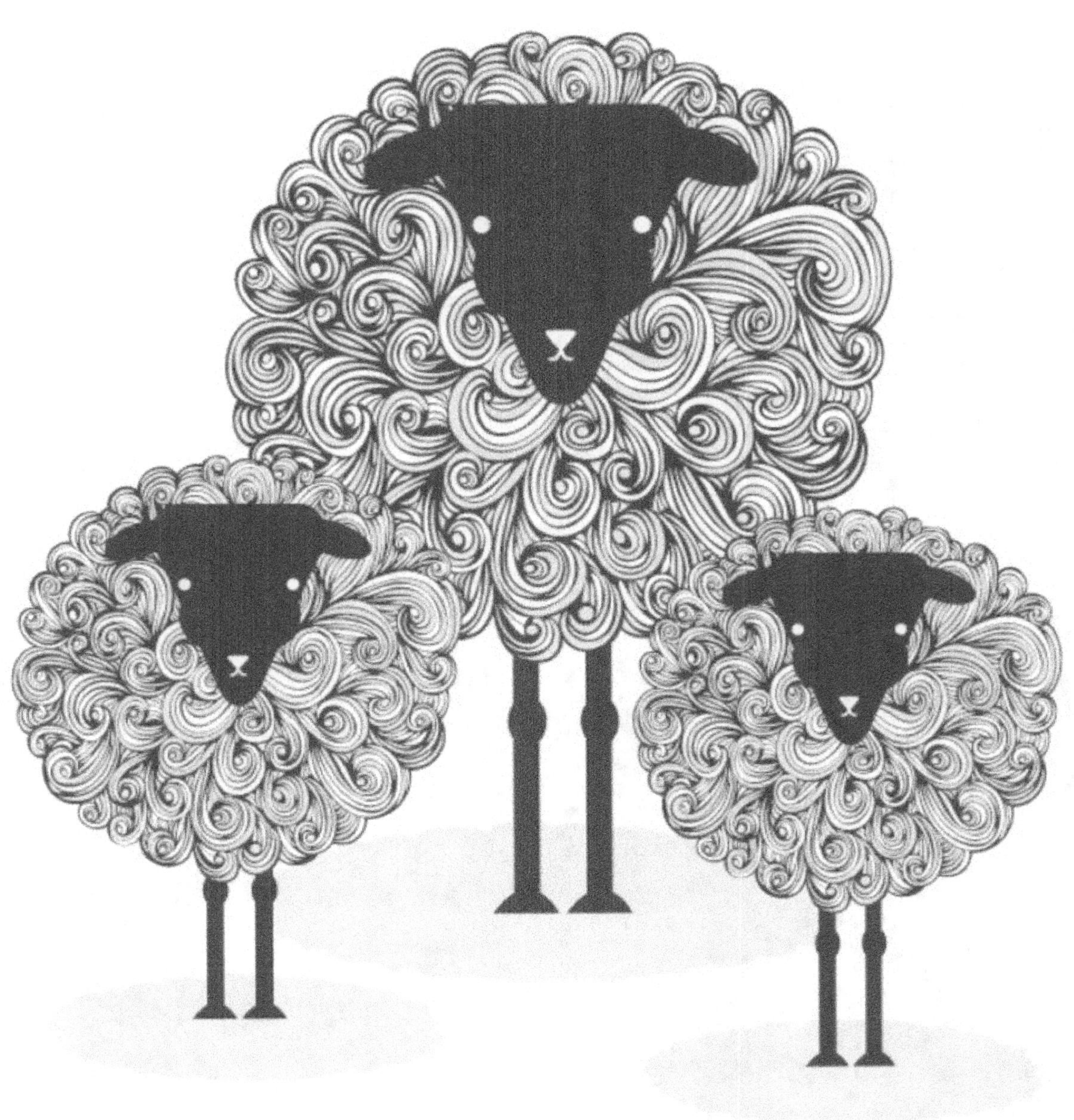

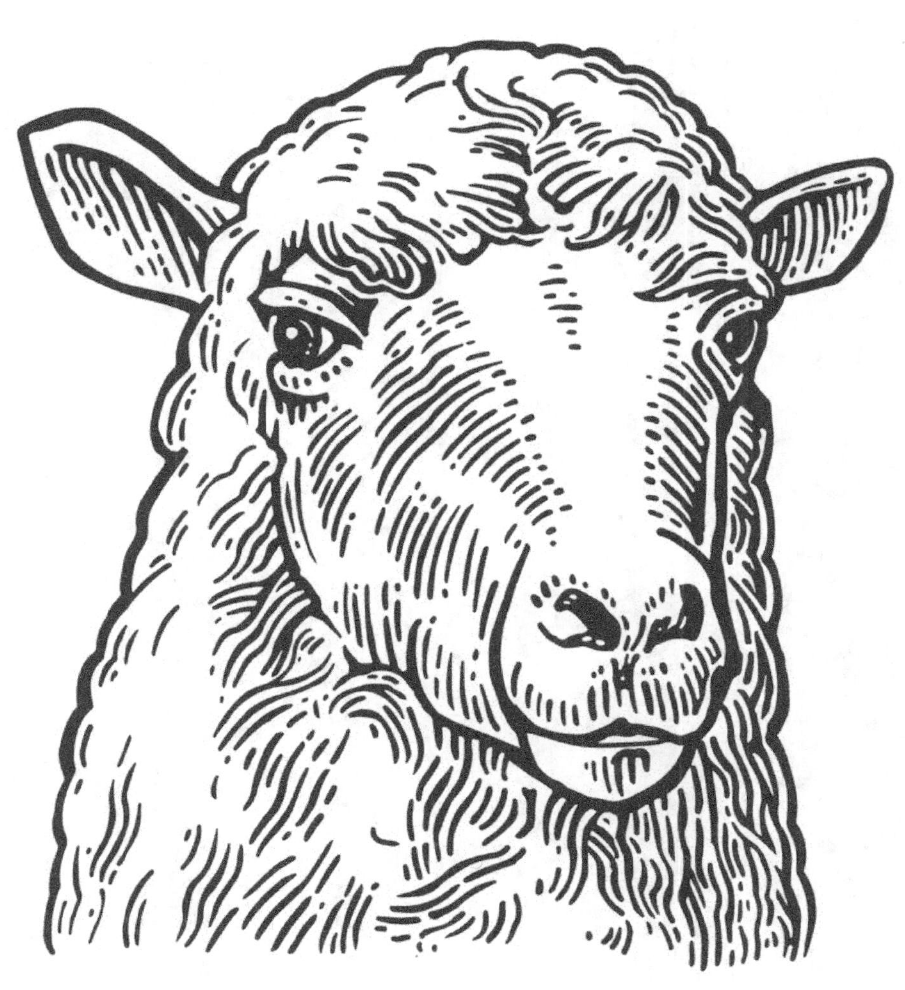

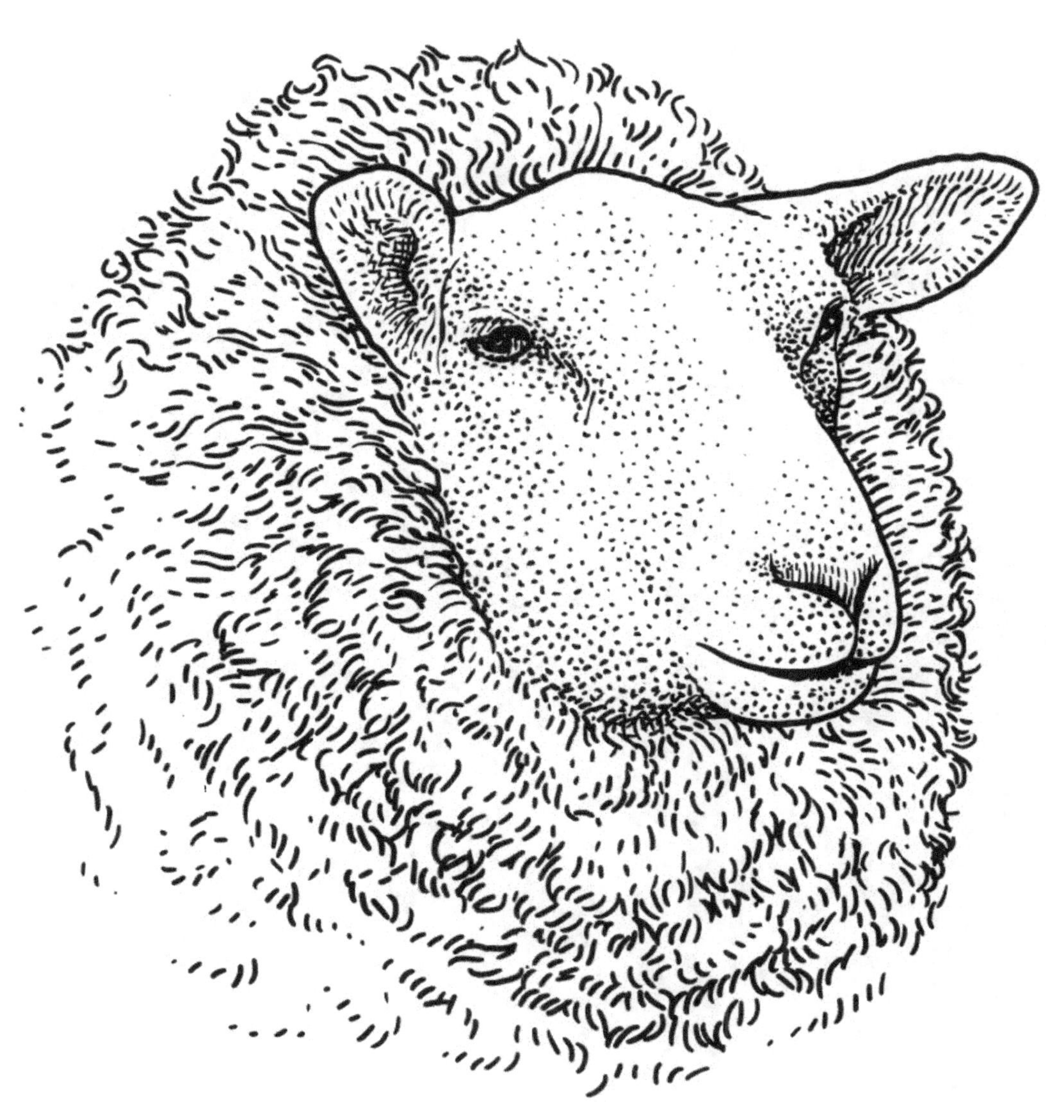

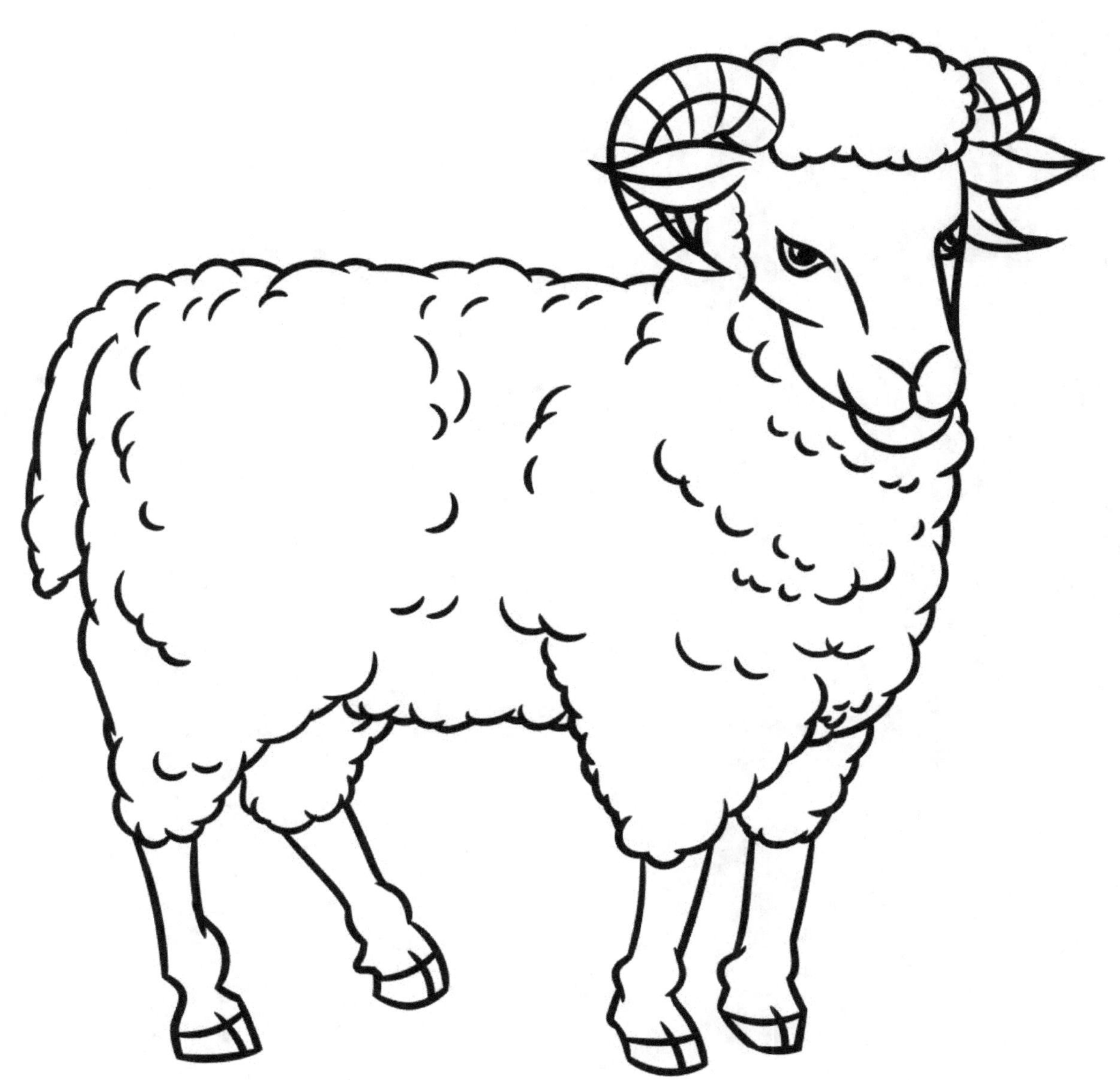

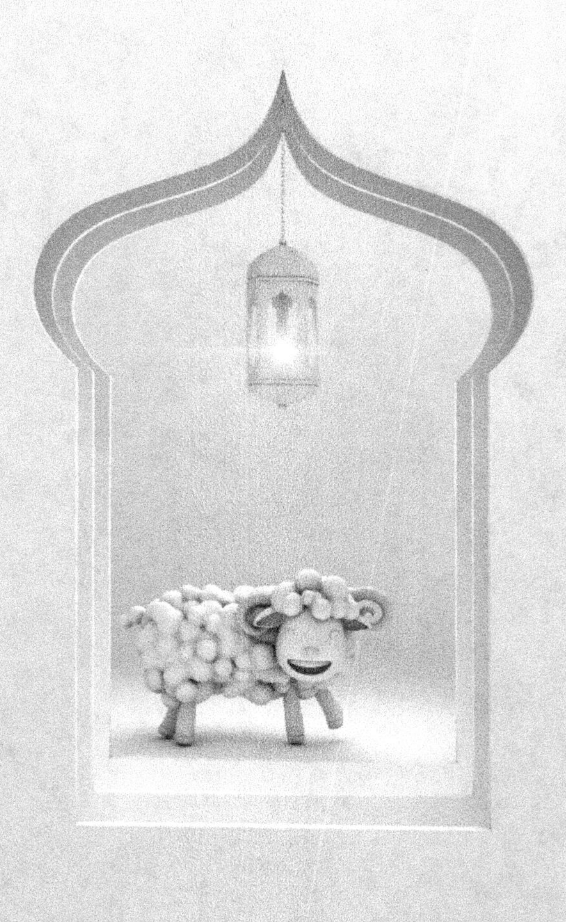

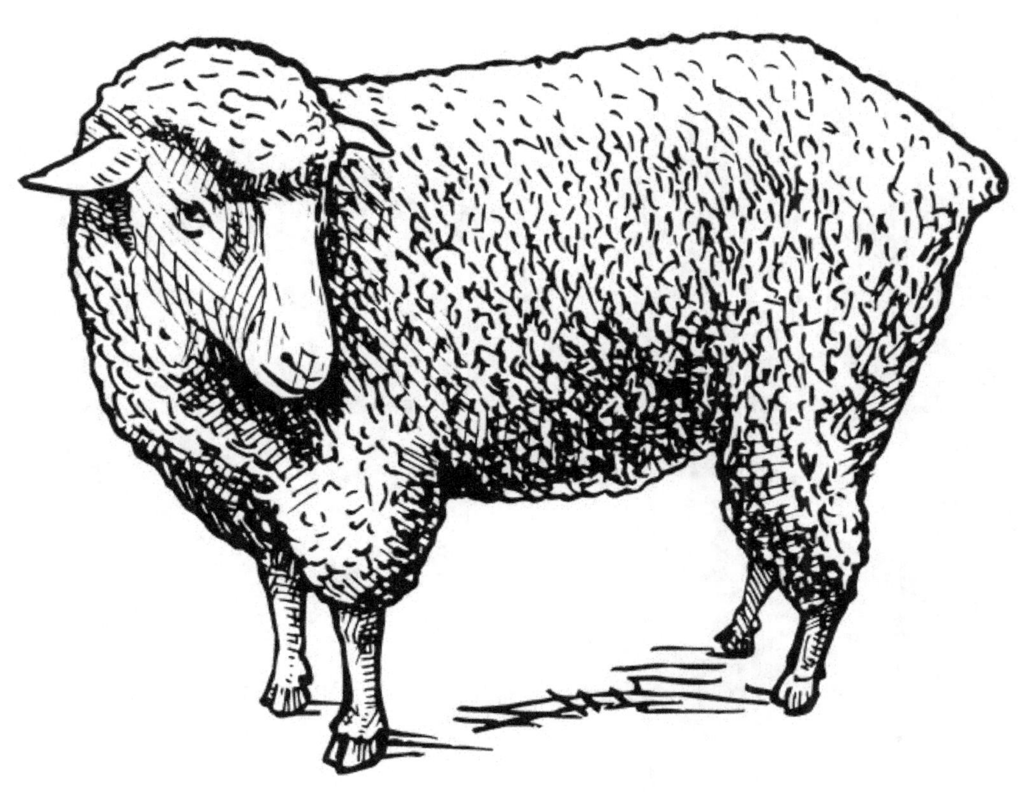

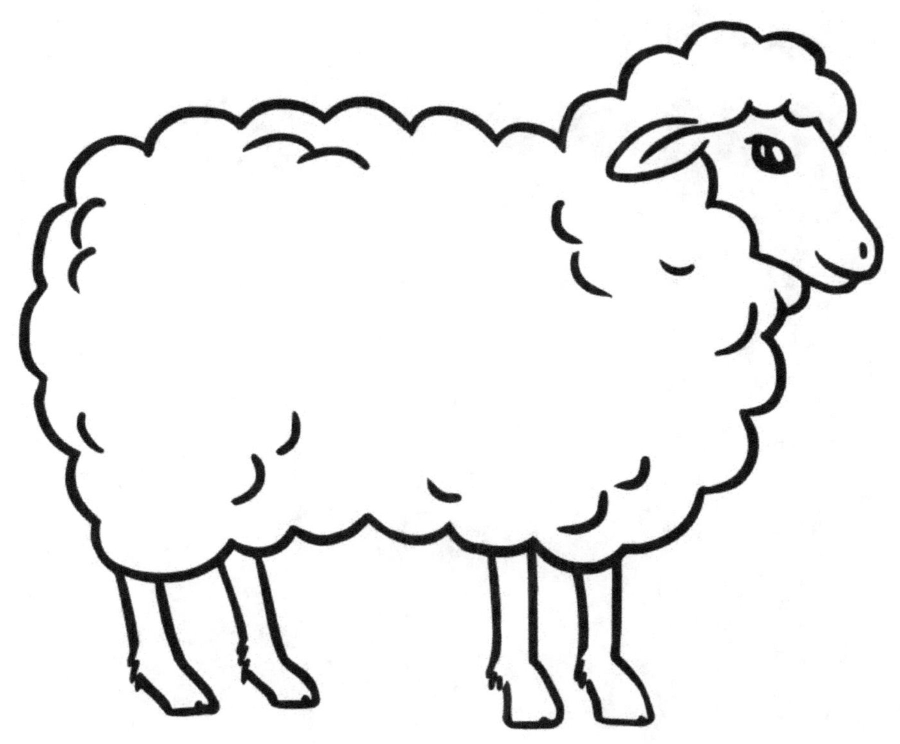

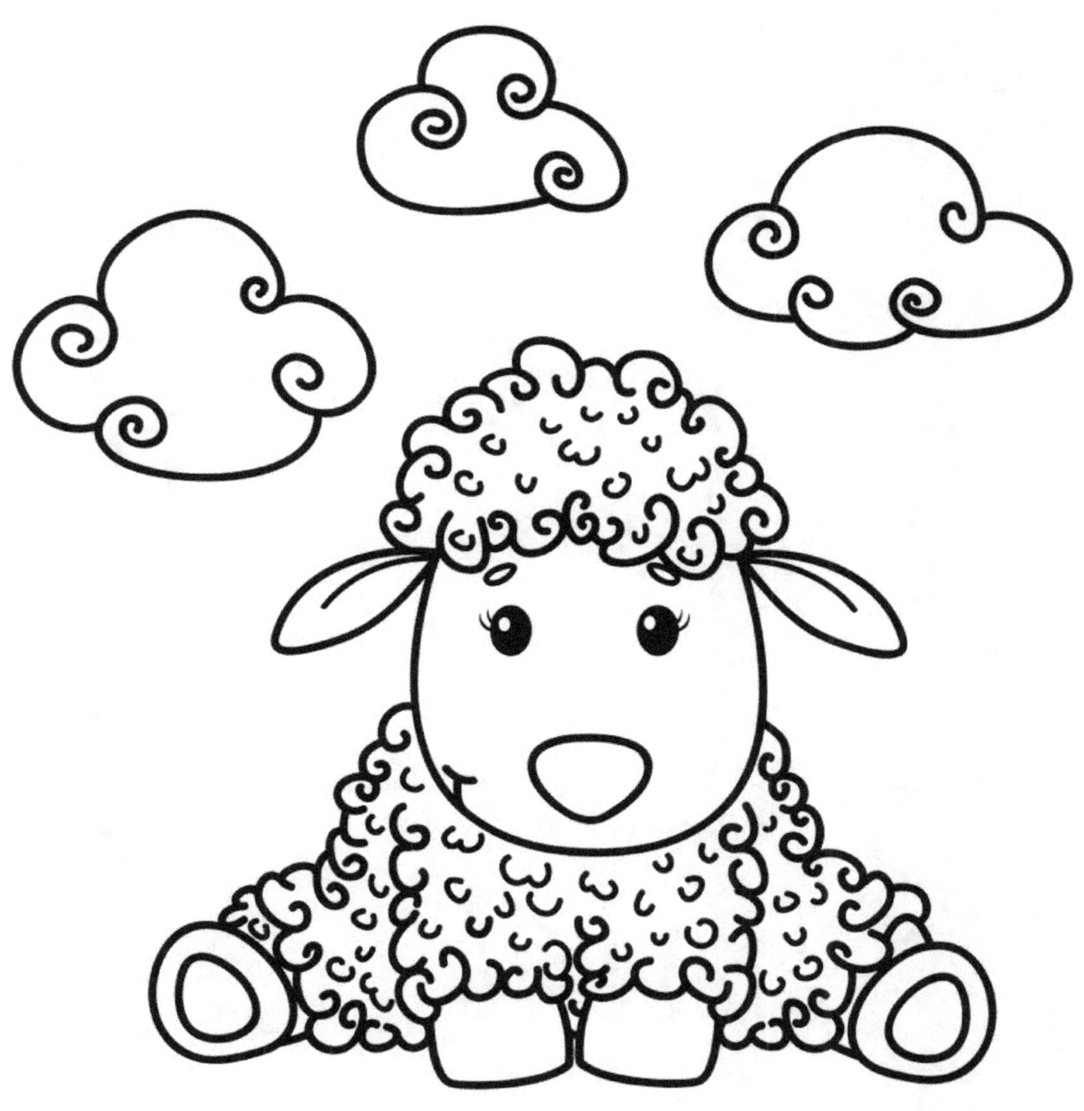

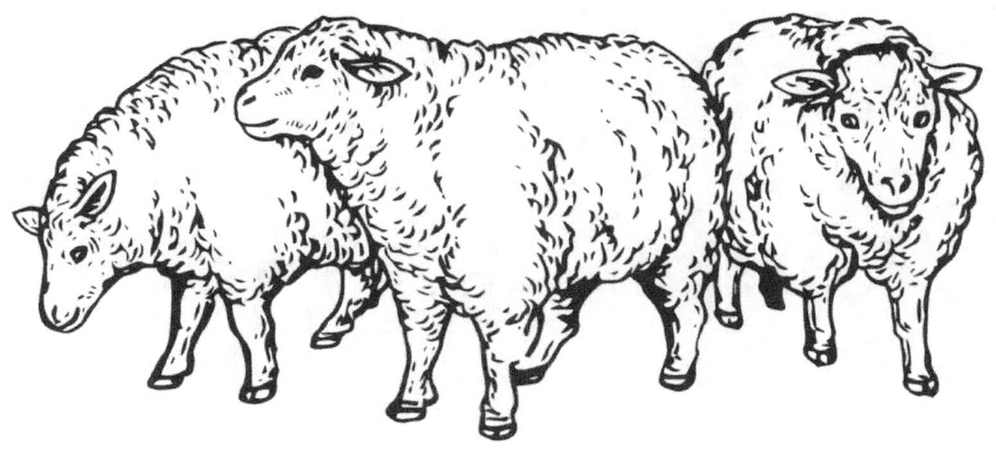

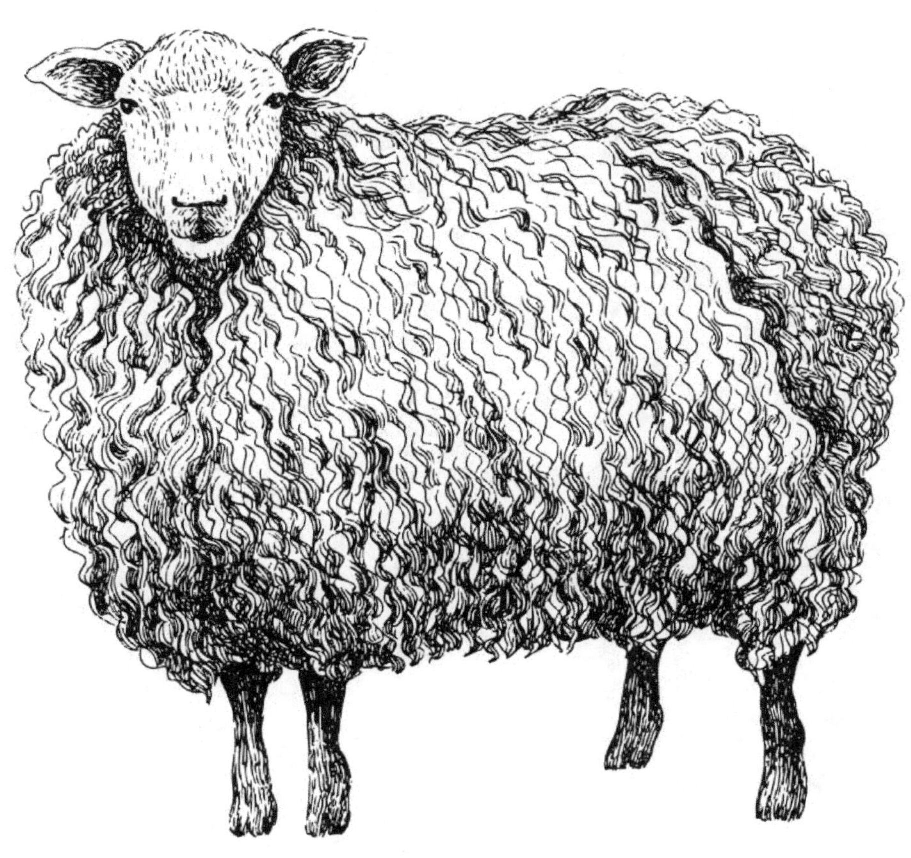

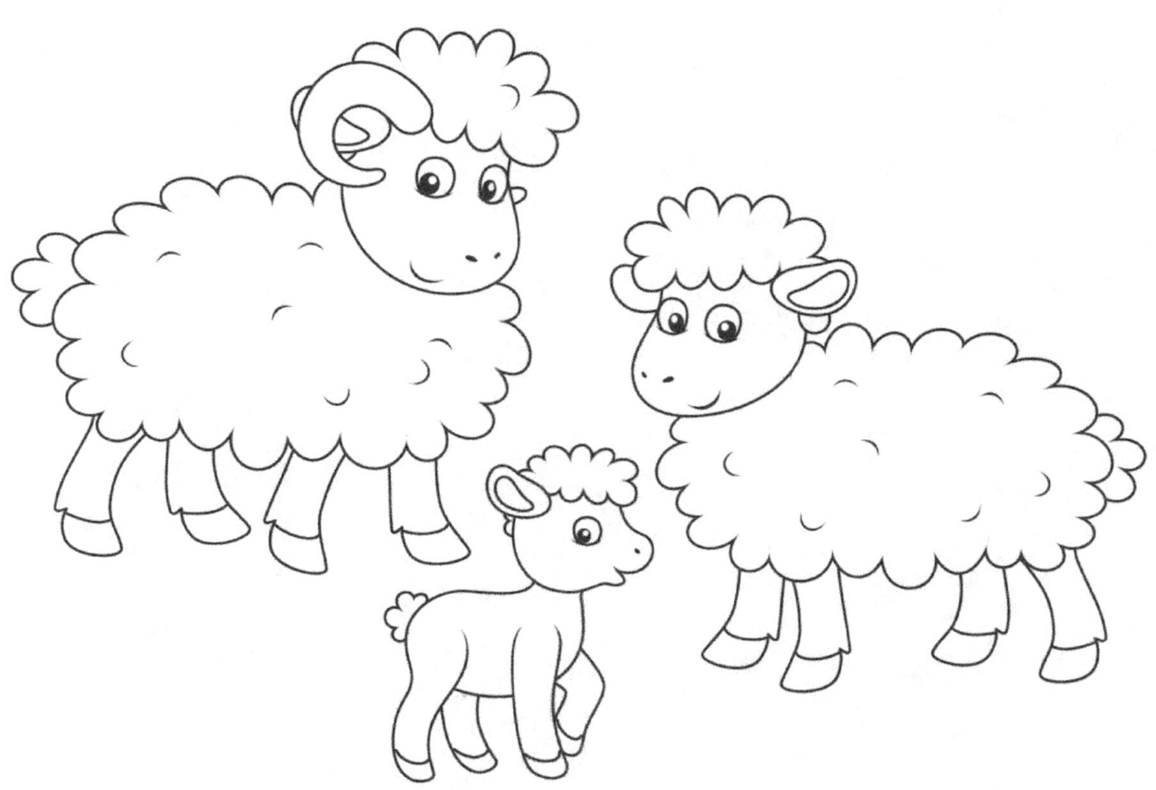

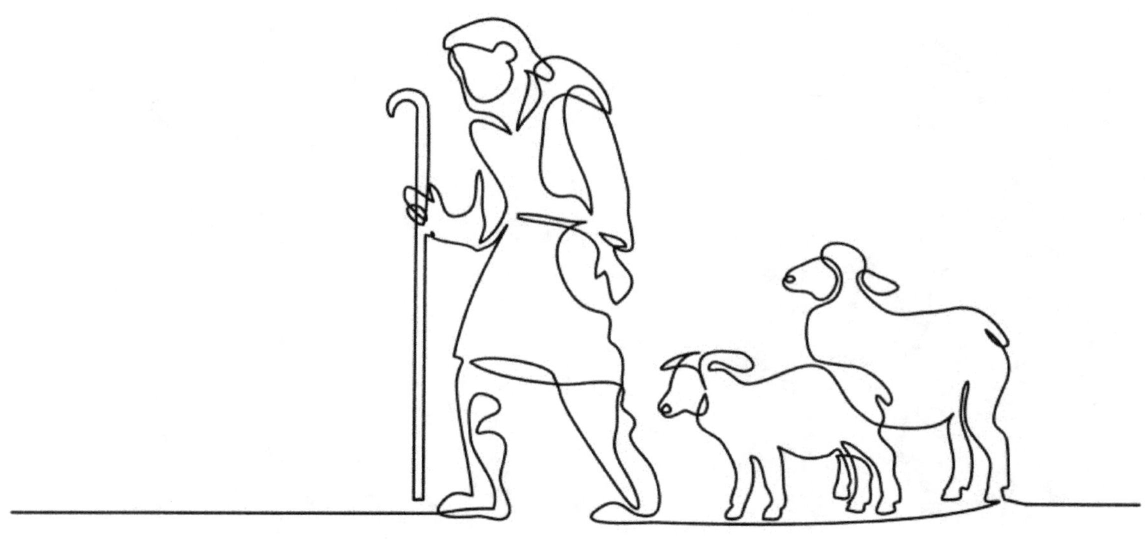

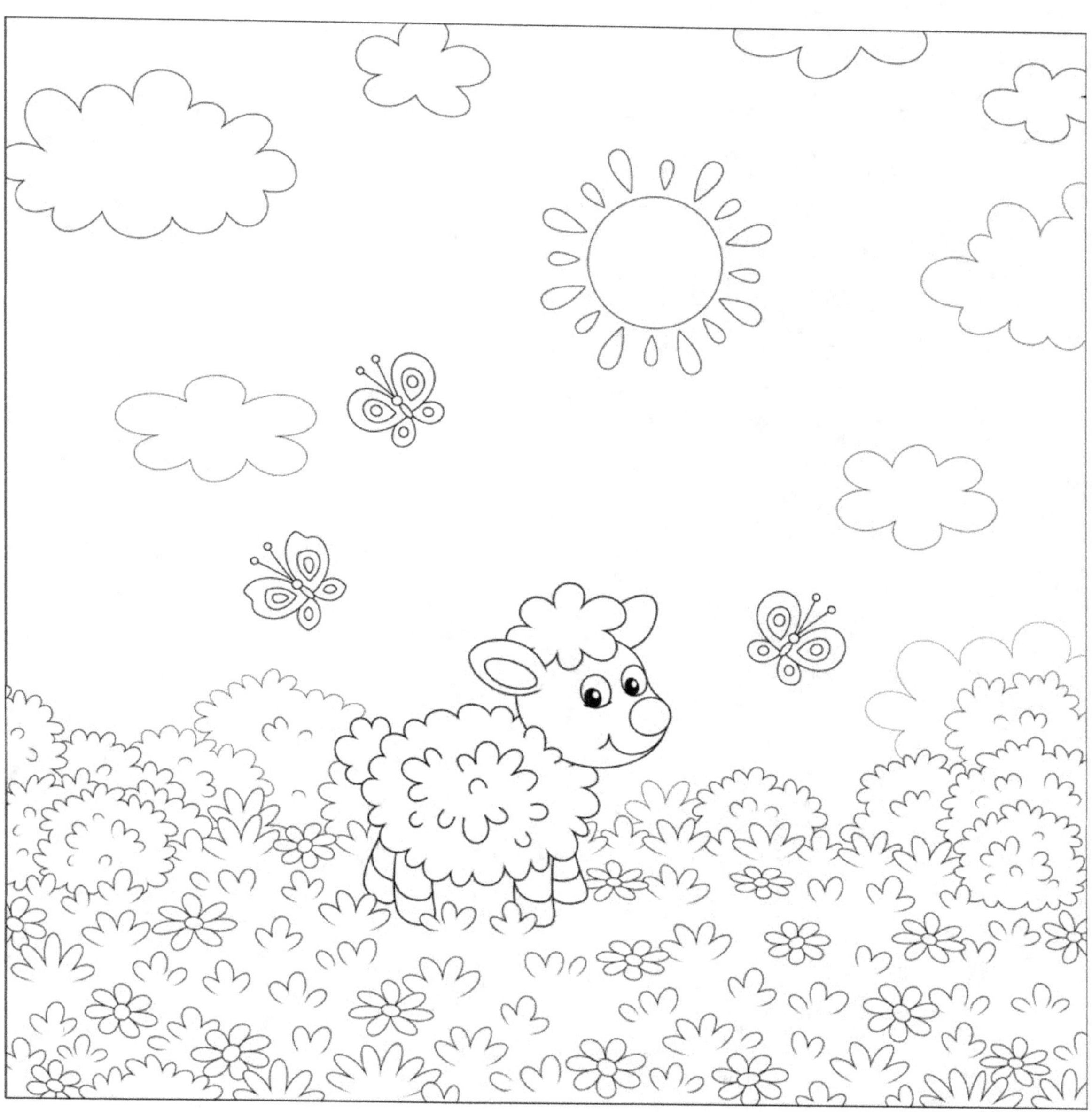

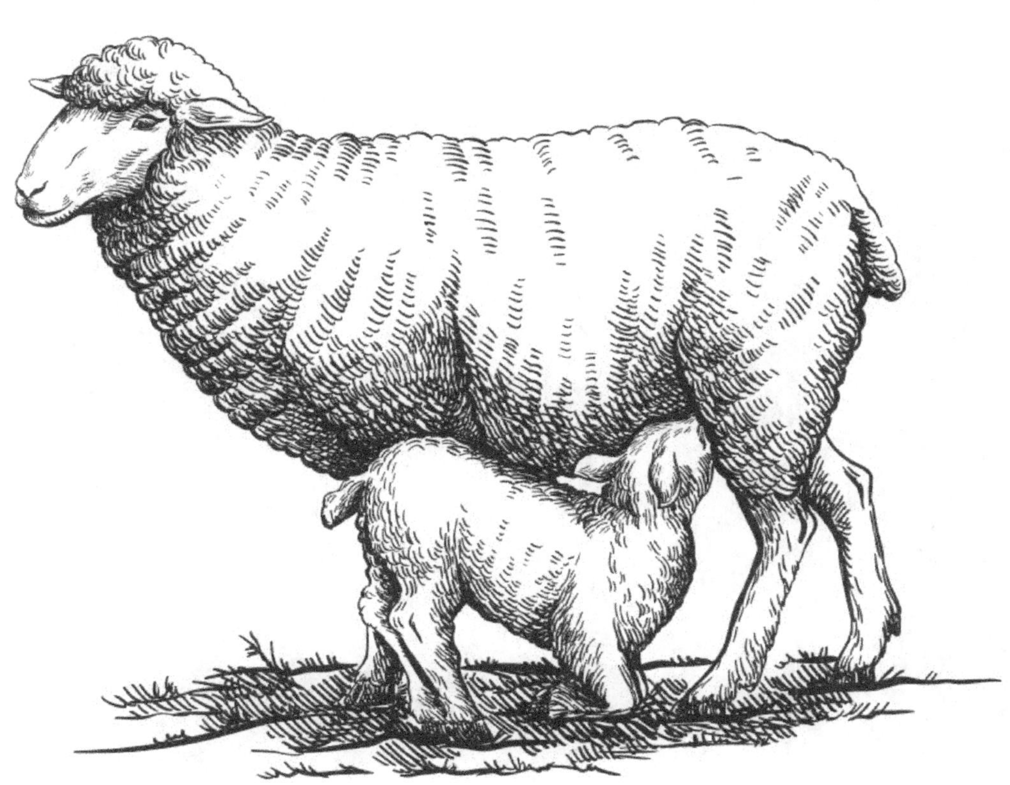

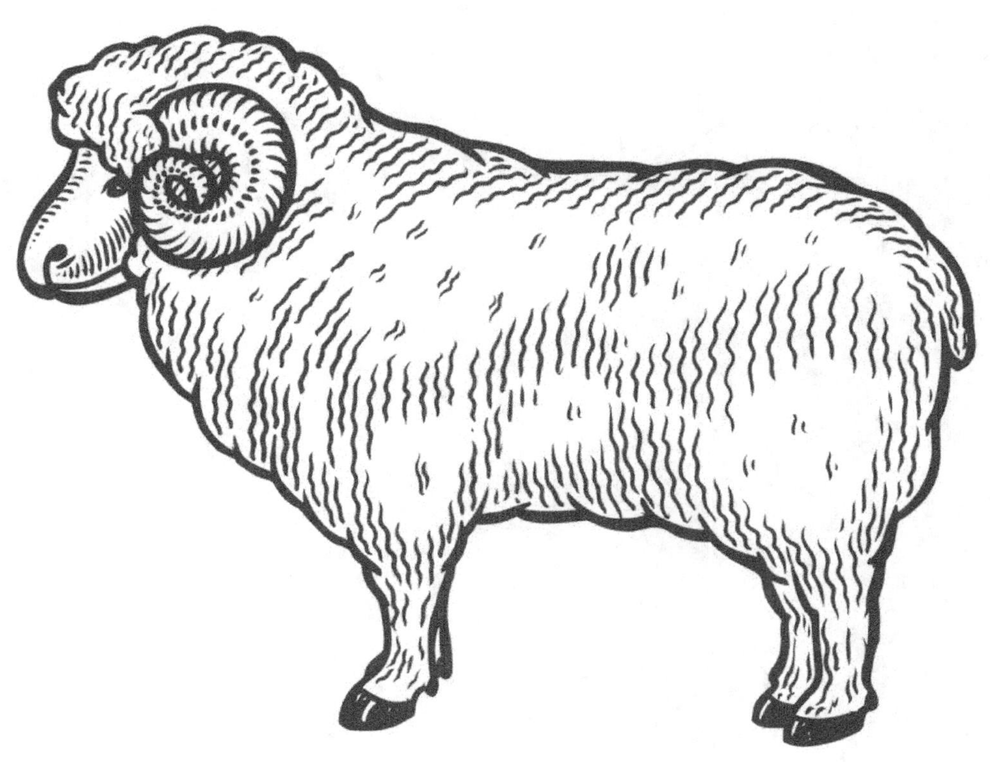

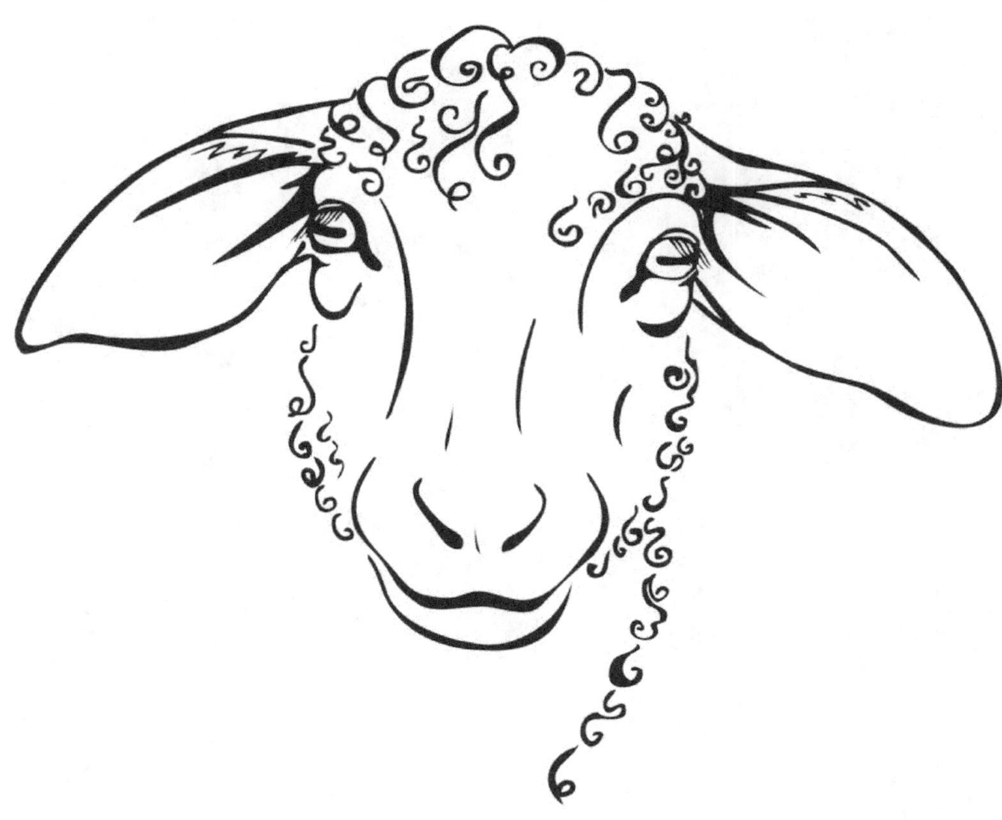

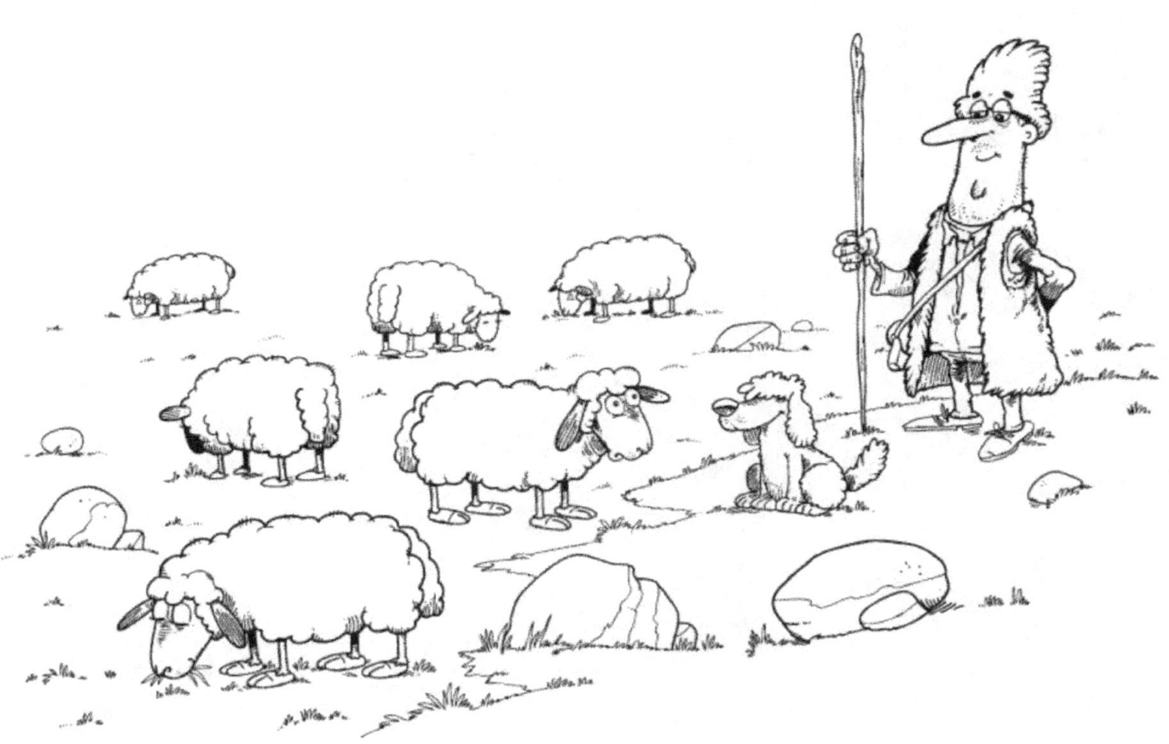

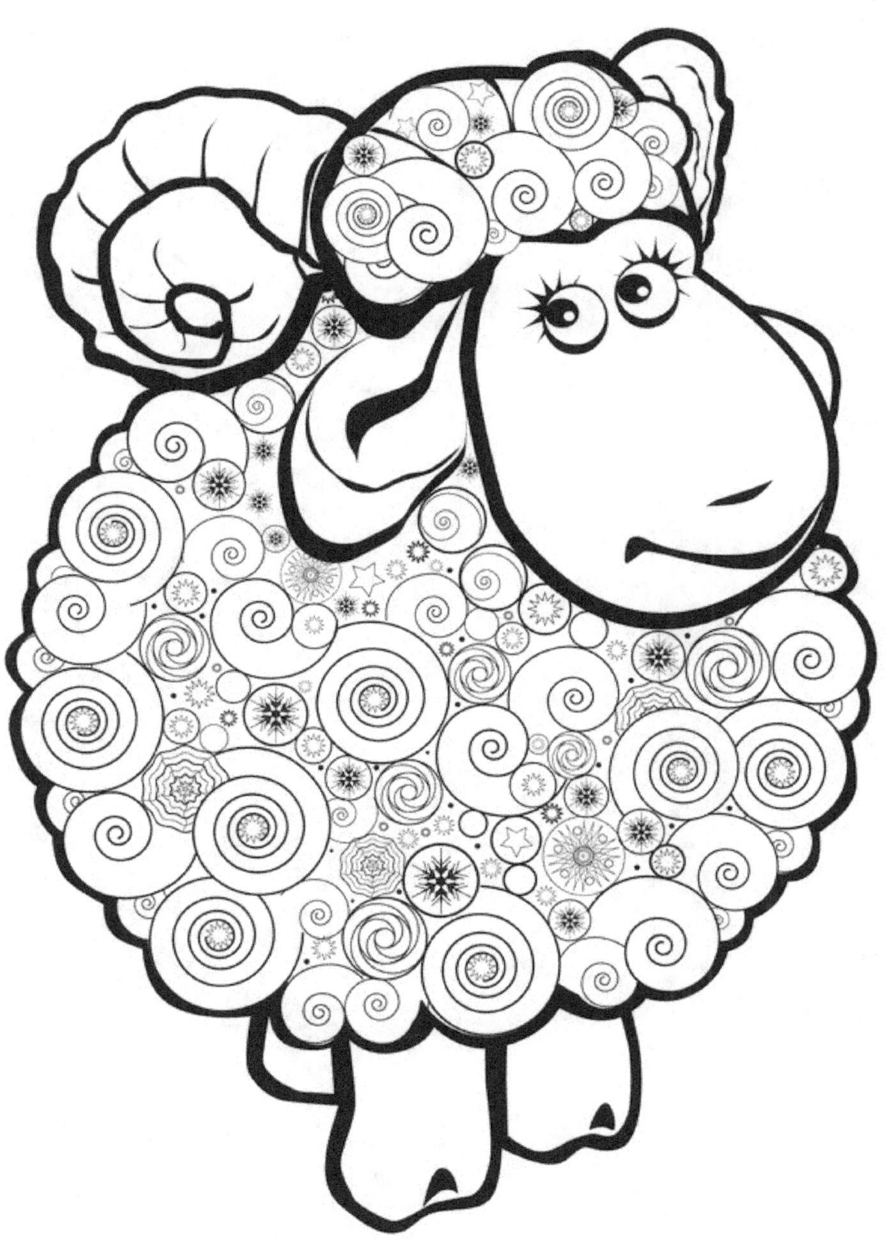

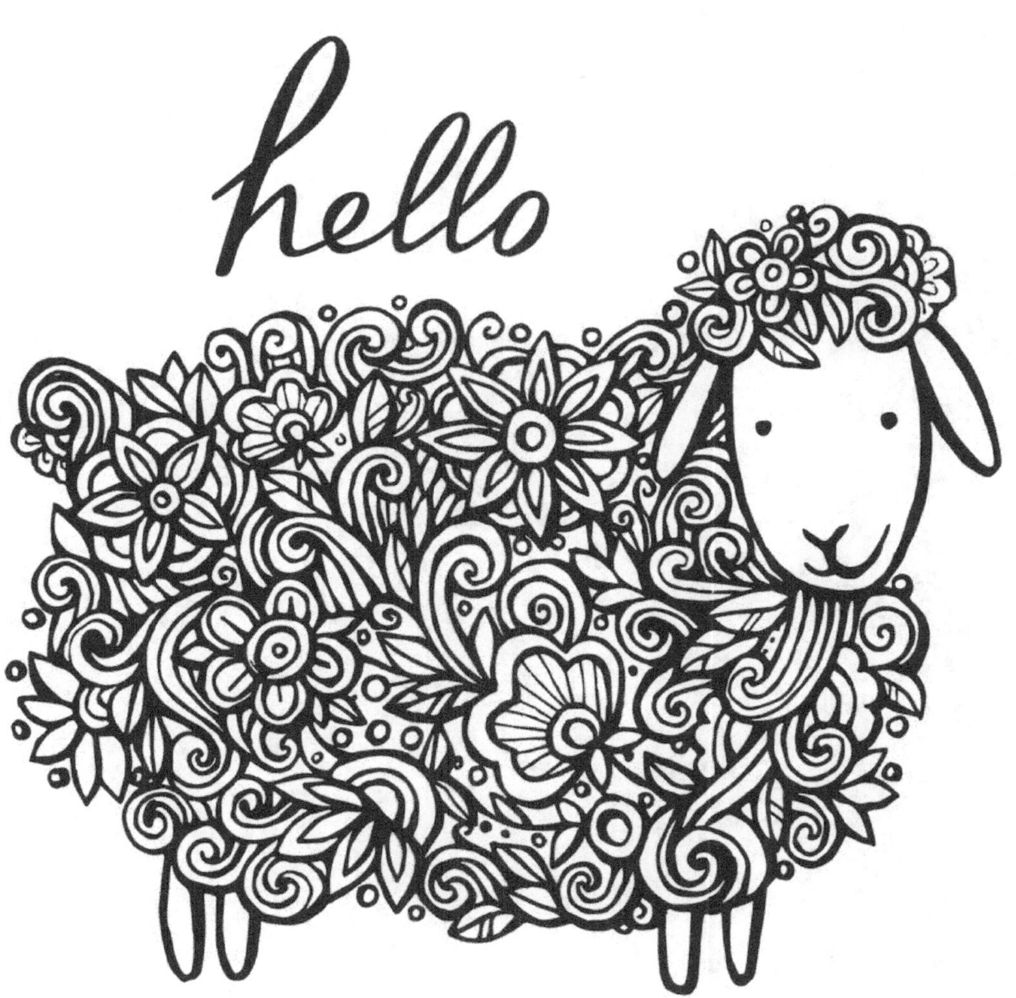
hello

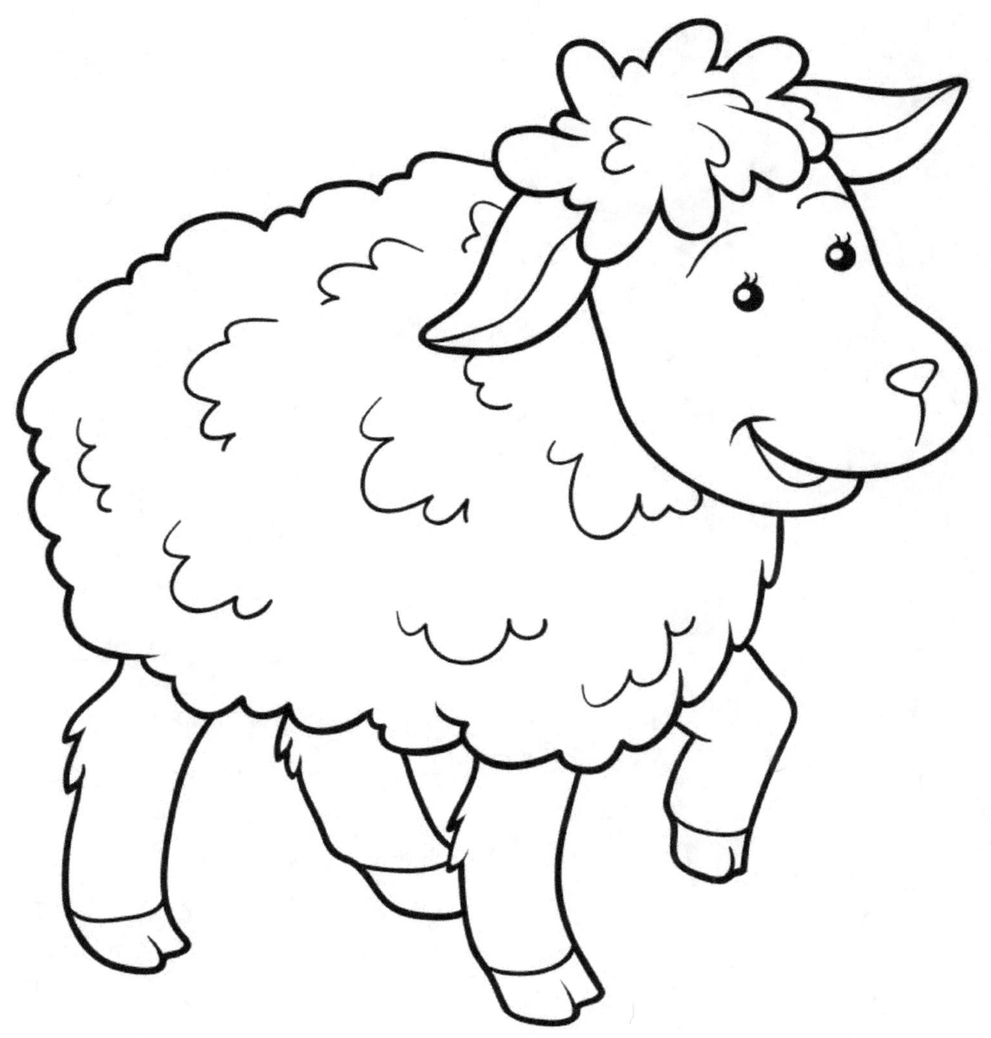

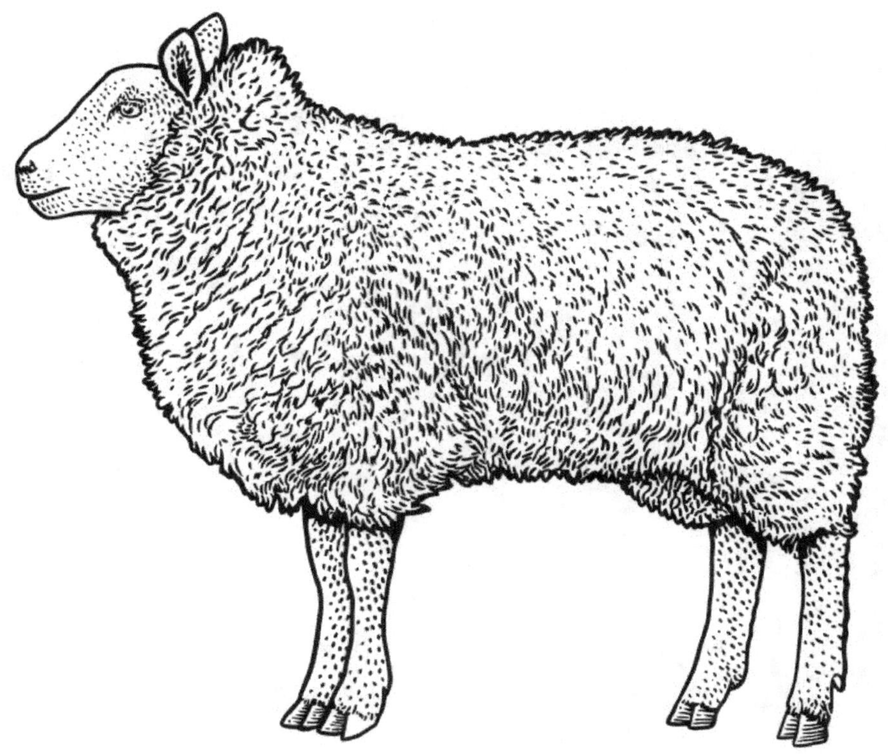

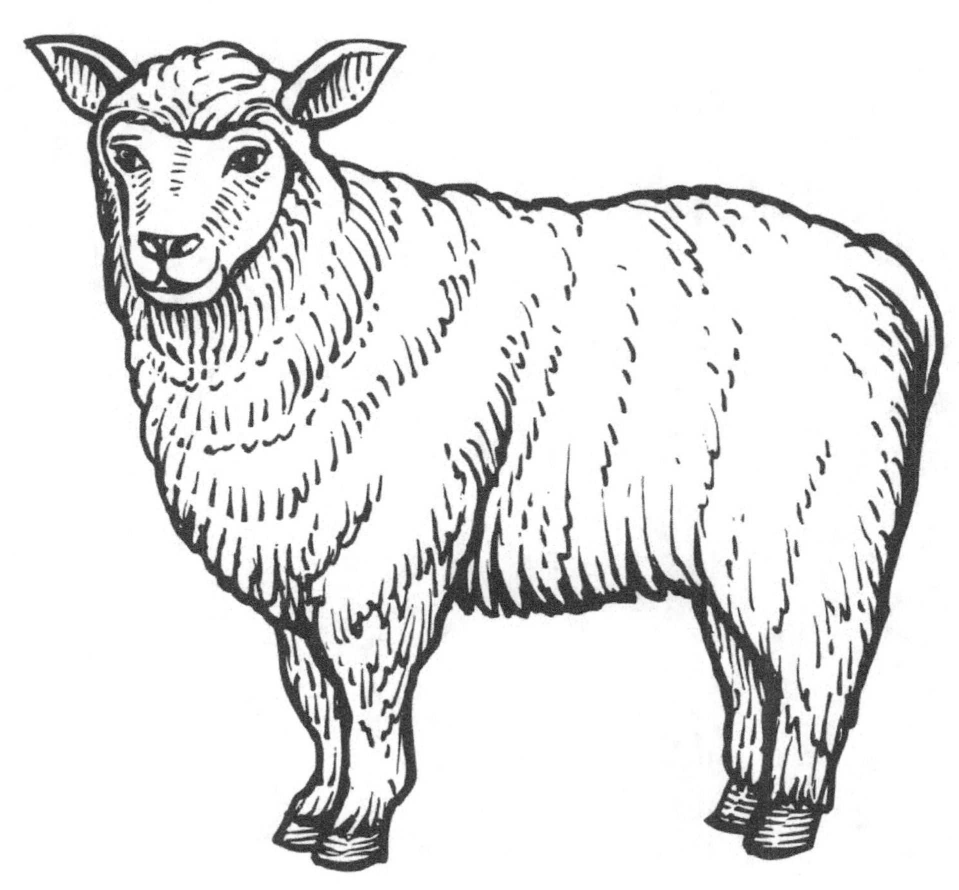

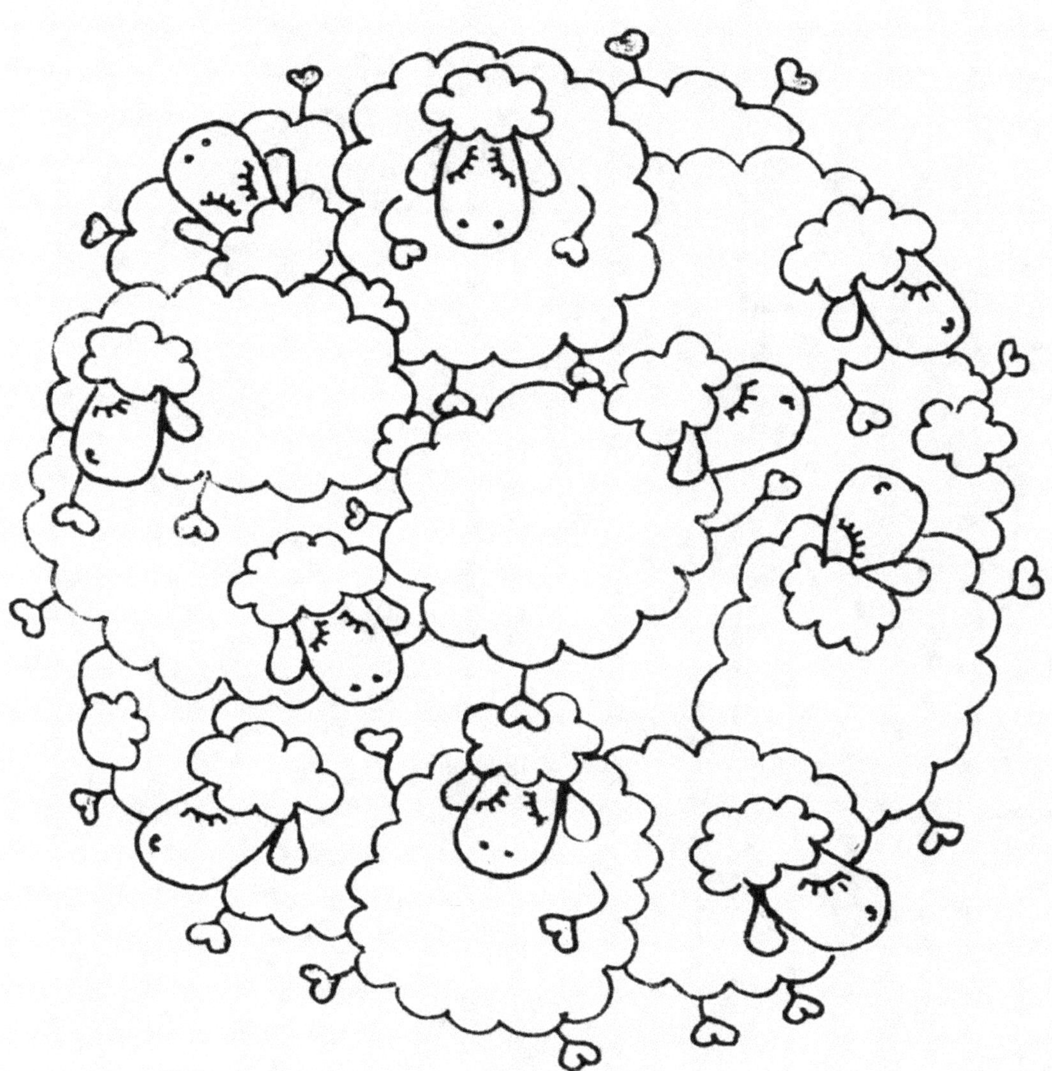

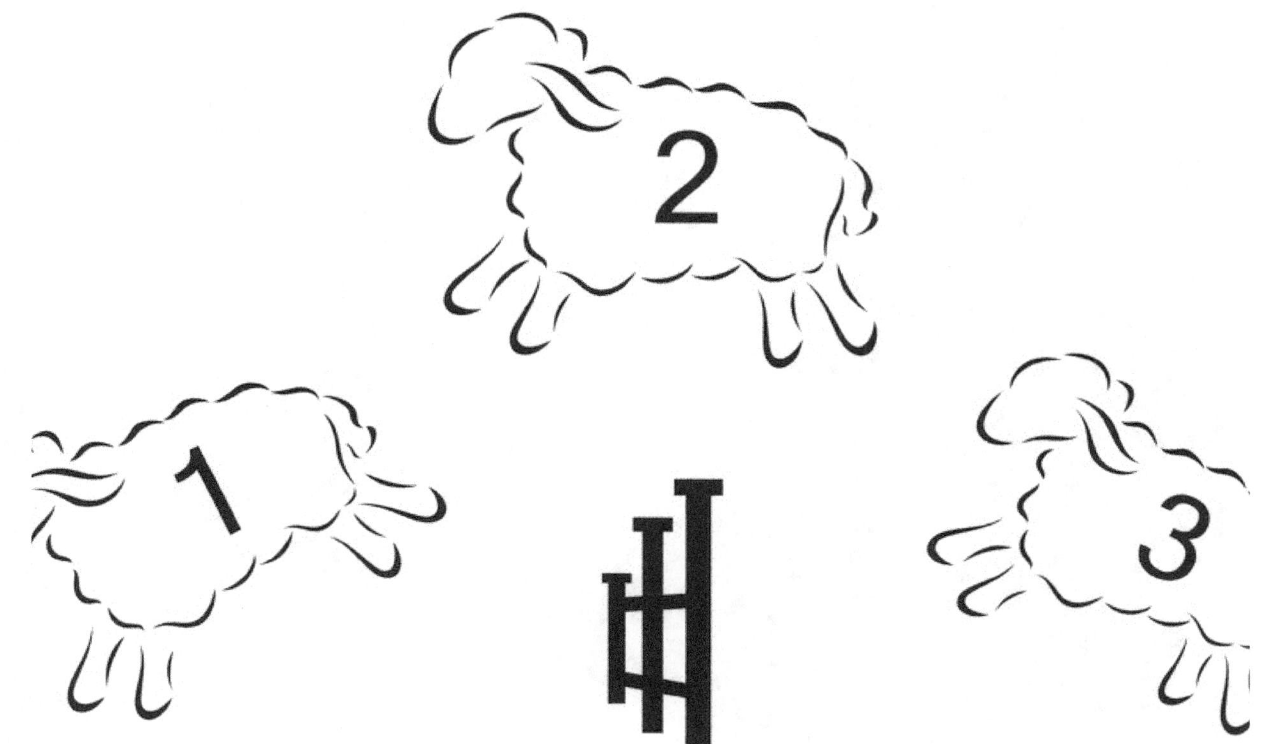

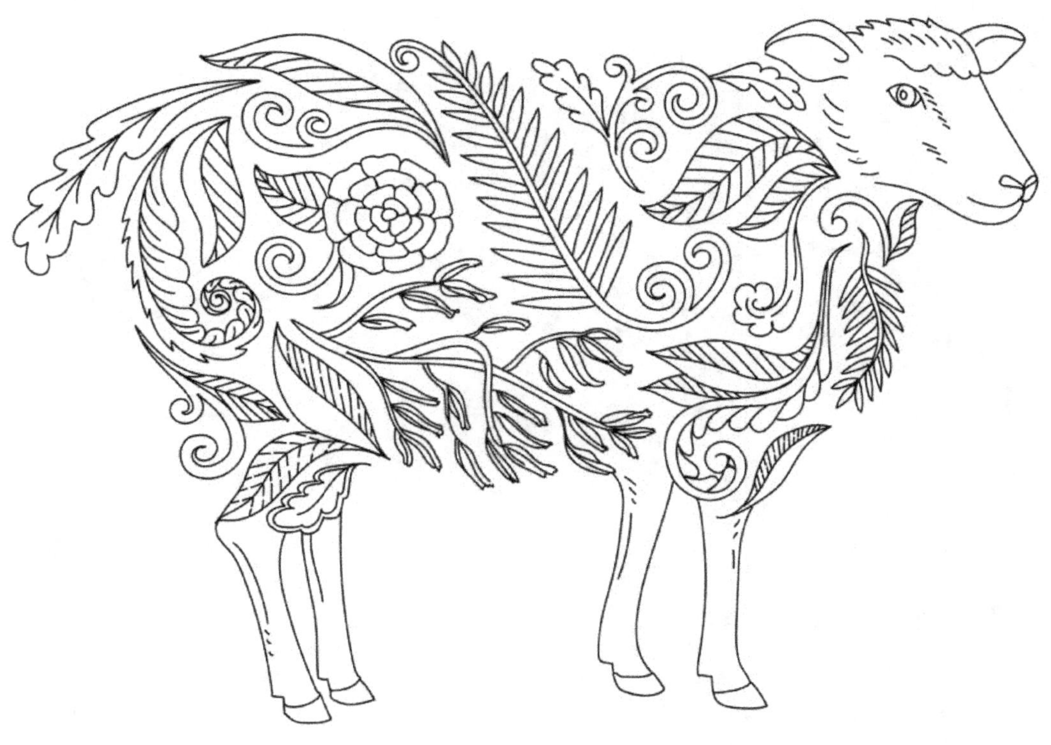

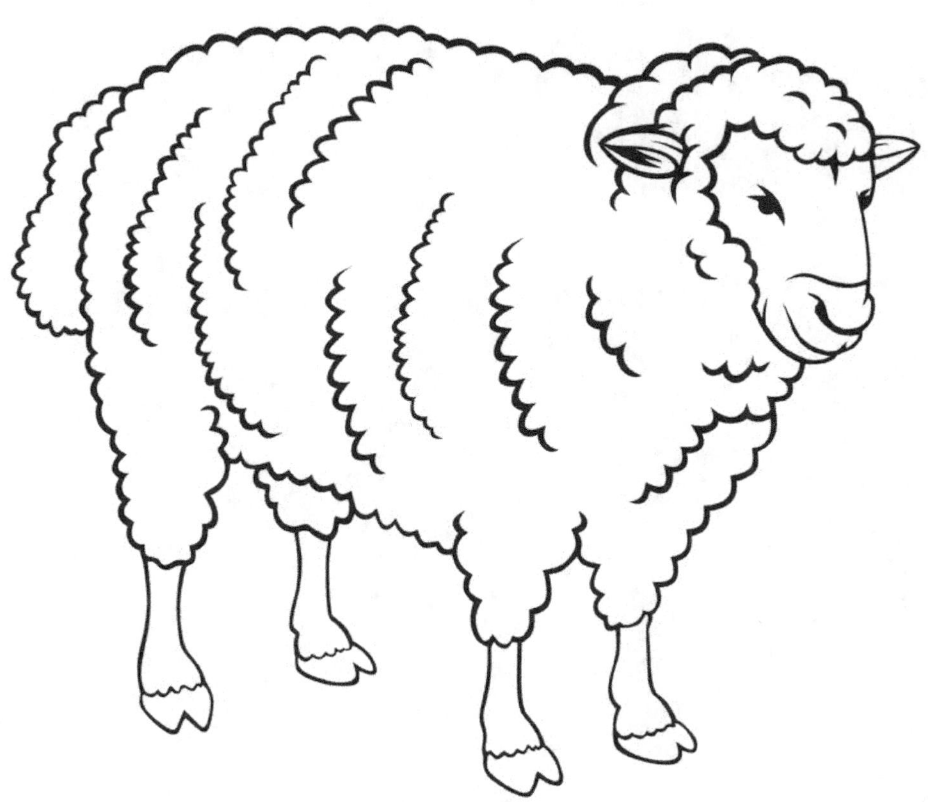

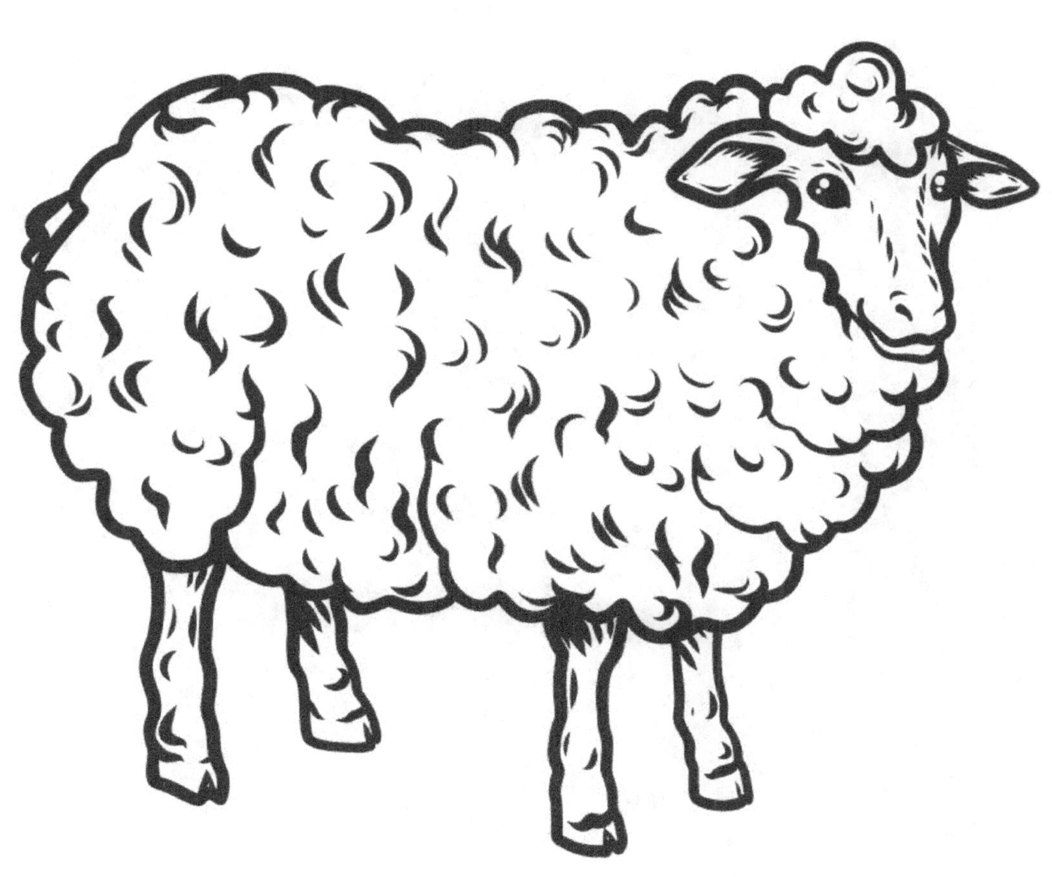

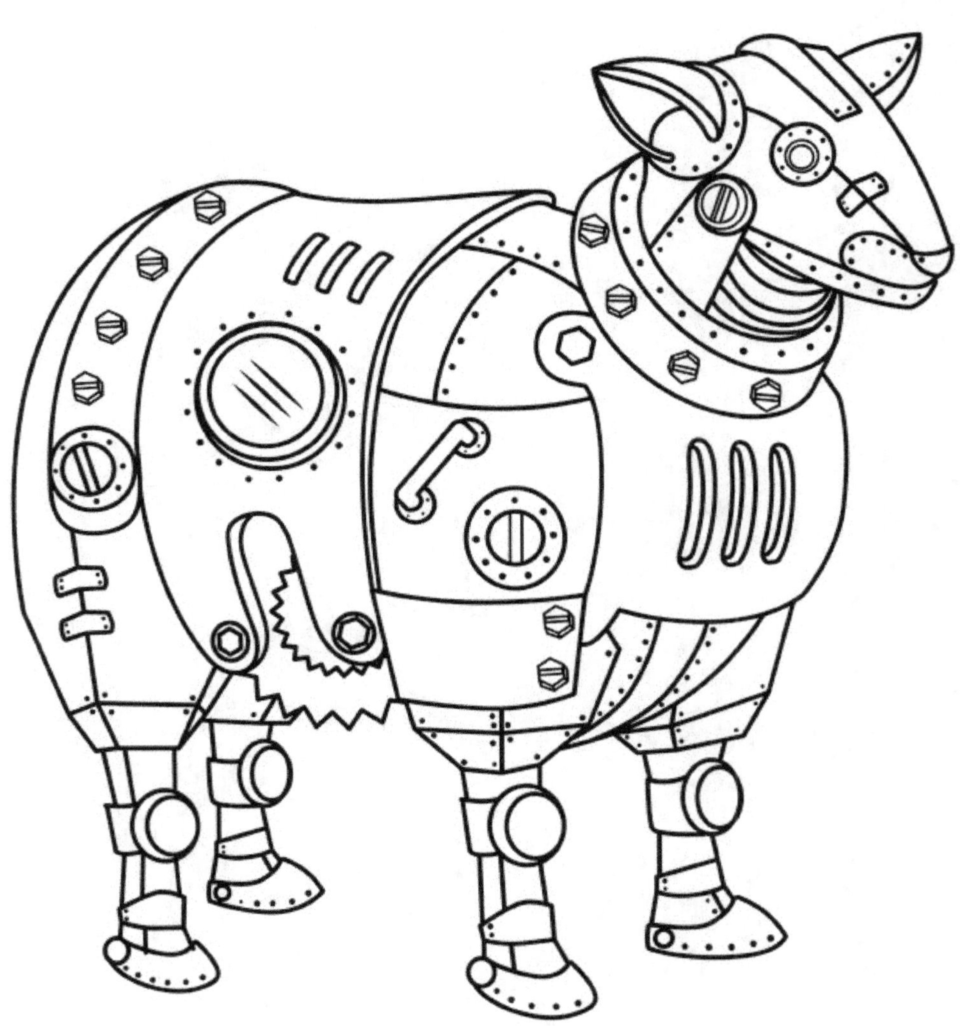

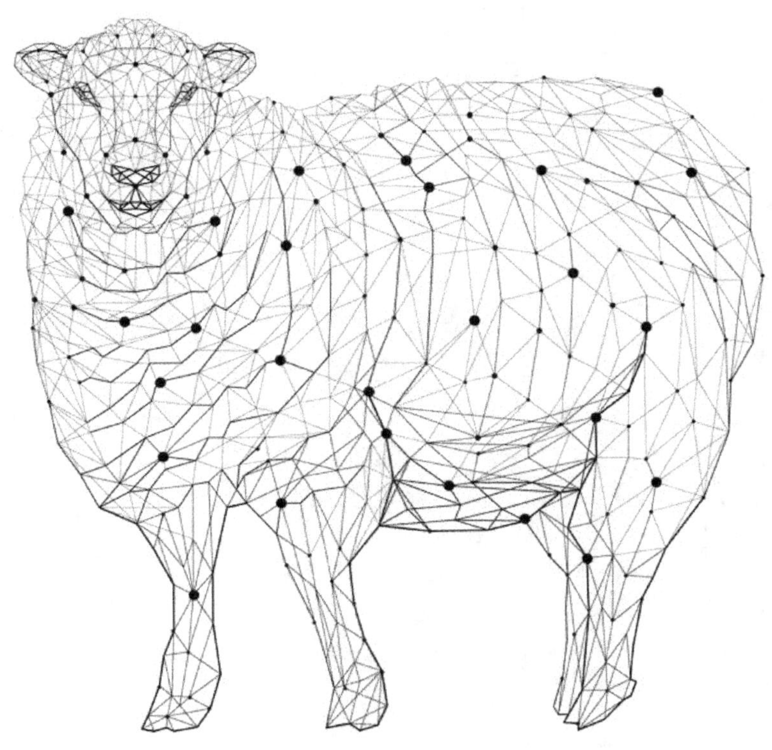

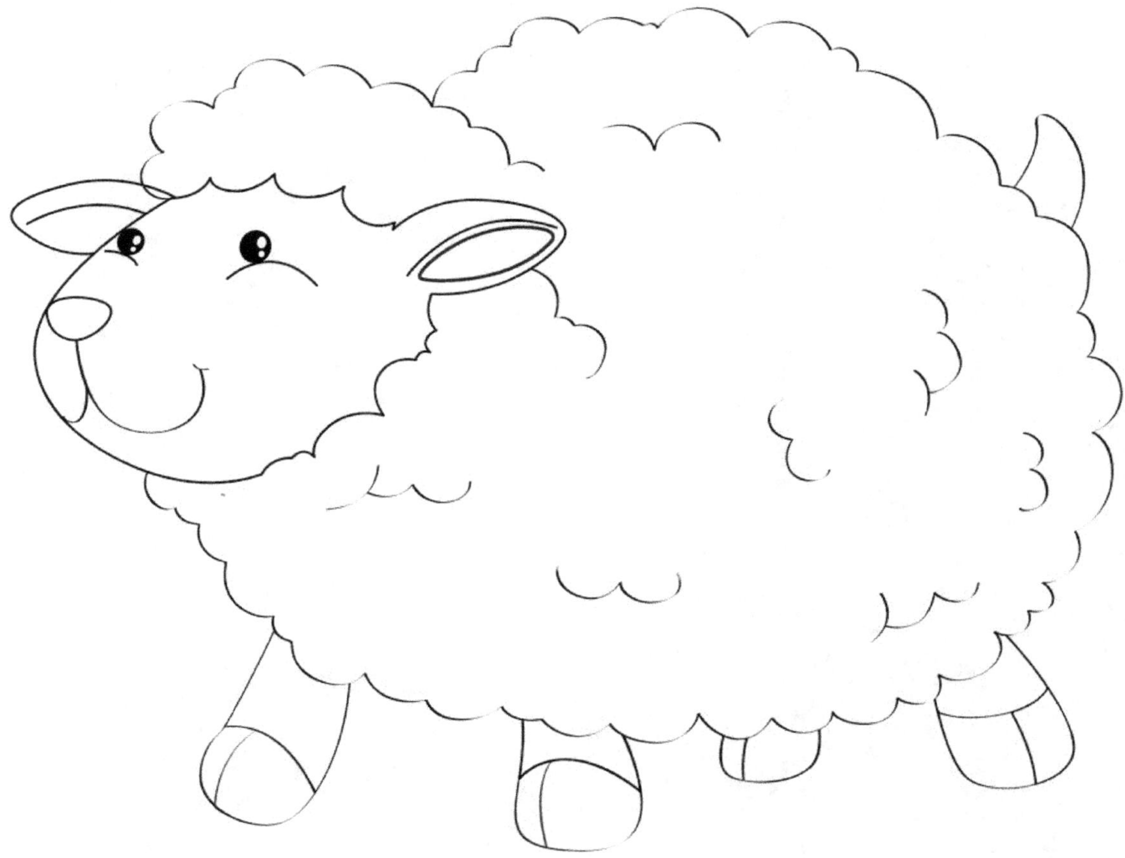

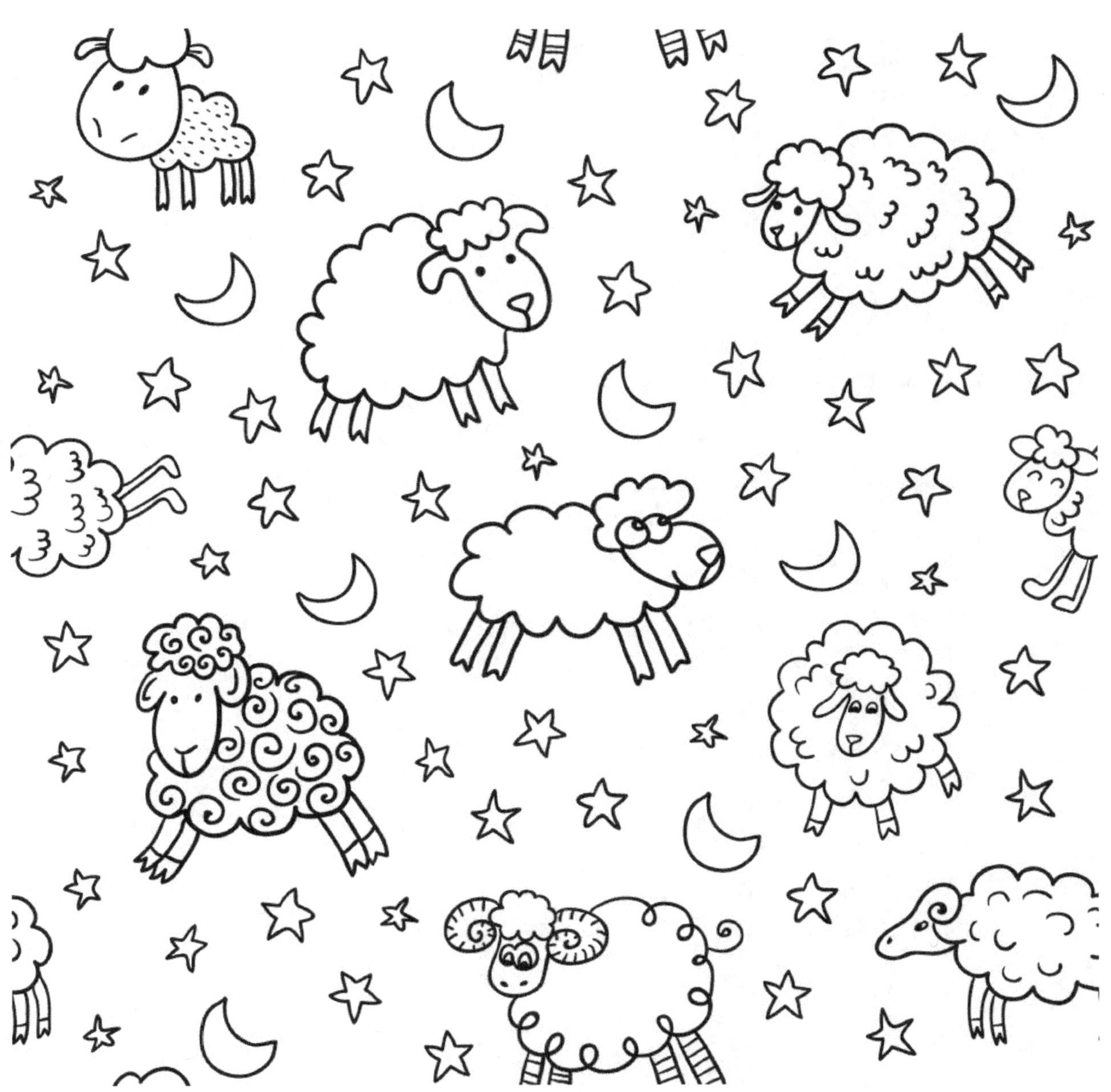